Isaiah 26:3-4

"PERFECT PEACE VII"

Isaiah 26:3-4

"PERFECT PEACE VII"
Eleven

Vanessa Rayner

authorHOUSE®

AuthorHouse™
1663 Liberty Drive
Bloomington, IN 47403
www.authorhouse.com
Phone: 1-800-839-8640

Published by AuthorHouse   10/29/2014

ISBN: 978-1-4969-4810-6 (sc)
ISBN: 978-1-4969-4809-0 (e)

Scripture quotations marked KJV are from the Holy Bible, King James
Version (Authorized Version). First published in 1611. Quoted from the KJV
Classic Reference Bible, Copyright © 1983 by The Zondervan Corporation.

Scripture quotations marked NLT are taken from the Holy
Bible, New Living Translation, copyright © 1996, 2004,
2007. Used by permission of Tyndale House Publishers, Inc.
Carol Stream, Illinois 60188. All rights reserved. Website

A GIFT . . .

*P*resented to

_____

*F*rom

_____

*D*ate

_____

WHEN LIFE GETS TOO
HARD TO STAND;
KNEEL

CONTENTS

THEME

Perfect Peace for your mind, spirit, soul and body is the message and purpose of this book. Isaiah 26:3-4 series is concerning God's Perfect Peace. This is the distinct and unifying composition of this book with the subtitle <u>Eleven</u>.

Thou wilt keep him in perfect peace, whose mind is stayed on thee: because he trusteth in thee. Trust ye in the LORD for ever: for in the LORD JEHOVAH is everlasting strength. These verses are from Isaiah 26:3-4, the King James Version (KJV) known as the "Word for Word Translation."

You will keep in perfect peace all who trust in you, all whose thoughts are fixed on you! Trust in the Lord always, for the Lord God is the eternal Rock. These verses are from Isaiah 26:3-4, the New Living Testament (NLT) known as the "Paraphrase Translation."

DO YOU KNOW THE DIFFERENT?

NOTE: The "Word for Word" and "Paraphrase" Translations, along with the Thought for Thought Translation are explained in details in the book titled

Isaiah 26:3-4, "Perfect Peace" <u>The Last Single Digit</u>, Chapter 1.

Make an effort to jot down the different, in Jesus' Name:

_____

_____

_____

_____

_____

_____

_____

_____

_____

_____

PRAYER

O Father God, in the Name of Jesus,
I pray that this book will help everyone who read it
In a profound way.
Father, I pray that it will even bless
those who just read the title,
Or look at it, or picks it up briefly.

Father God, I thank You for those that help make
Your Work and Word able to go
forth in a sin-sick world.

Father, You make it clear that You will
reward those that bless your servant.
It could be by prayer, words of
encourage, buying a book,
e-mailing or twittering others about the book,
to even given that person a cup of water.

**And if you give even a cup of cold water
to one of the least of my followers,
You will surely be rewarded.**
Matthew 10:42 NLT

Father, I ask now that You continue
to give me strength,
to continue my journey, to keep doing Your work
Regardless of the road blocks, wrong
turns, pot holes and road detours.
I thank You for
Your mercy, Your grace, and Your
faithful love which endures forever.

Father, I give you all the Glory, Praise, and
Honor because You are so Worthy.

Amen.

AUTHOR'S NOTES

Author notes normally provide a way to add extra information to one's book that may be awkward and inappropriate to include in the text of the book itself. It provides supplemental contextual details on the aspects of the book. It can help readers understand the book content and the background details of the book better. The times and dates of researching, reading, and gathering this information are not included; mostly when I typed on it.

June 10, 2013 ~ 0123

July 24, 2013 ~ 0137

July 28, 2013 ~ 0822

August 23, 2013 ~ 0410

August 29, 2013 ~ 0521

September 5, 2013 ~ 2032; I have been on Missionary Donella Pierce Chambers 16 hour prayer line today, which started at 0600 PST (0800 CST my time). Another book title was revealed to me around 1600 CST; "16." Hallelujah.

Just realized, I need to work on Zaccheaus first.

November 11, 2013 ~ 0933; I have been working on Zaccheaus this morning, also. I just can't get chapter 3 to read right; agree with my soul. I decided to take a break from it.

January 25, 2014 ~ 1921; I started proofreading over Zaccheaus earlier, today.

January 26, 2014 ~ 1805

January 31, 2014 ~ 1730

February 1, 2014 ~ 2221

February 4, 2014 ~ 2255

February 5, 2014 ~ 1751

February 6, 2014 ~ 1719; My God! I have an awful painful crook in my neck that runs down into my shoulders. Help me Father God.

February 7, 2014 ~ 0651

February 8, 2014 ~ 1935

February 11, 2014 ~ 1915

February 16, 2014 ~ 2301; Sent Perfect Peace VI to AuthorHouse this evening. Hallelujah is the Highest Praise!

February 17, 2014 ~ 0429

February 18, 2014 ~ 2025

March 7, 2014 ~ 0557; I got three whole days off from O'Reilly. Praise God!

March 8, 2014 ~ 0920

March 9, 2014 ~1952

March 15, 2014 ~ 0833

March 23, 2014 ~ 0500

April 1, 2014 ~ 1944

April 19, 2014 ~ 0605

April 20, 2014 ~ 0548; Easter Sunday

May 5, 2014 ~ 1938

May 13, 2014 ~ 2nd Day on my New/Old Job, I'm Loving it Father God!

June 28, 2014 ~ 0514; Praise God! I feel great this morning.

July 29, 2014 ~ 0715

July 30, 2014 ~ 2316

July 31, 2014 ~ 0000

August 13, 2014 ~ 2232

August 14, 2014 ~ 0000

August 19, 2014 ~ 0338

August 20, 2014 ~ 2313

August 21, 2014 ~ 0000

August 24, 2014 ~ 0040

August 25, 2014 ~ 2337

August 26, 2014 ~ 2328

August 27, 2014 ~ 0000

September 23, 2014 ~ 2309

September 24, 2014 ~ 0000

September 25, 2014 ~ 2348

September 26, 2014 ~ 0000

September 27, 2014 ~ 0000

September 29, 2014 ~ 2245; Proofreading, I'm so glad, I'm at this point! Glory!

September 30, 2014 ~ 0000; Proofreading

October 1, 2014 ~ 0000; Proofreading

October 3, 2014 ~ 2027; Got off early tonight without asking; just what I needed. Thanks Father God & Lieutenant Mil . . . . .

October 8, 2014 ~ 23:11; Tonight the night. Praise God!

PREFACE

Isaiah 26:3-4, "Perfect Peace VII" ~ Eleven

This book is the 7th book of a series of Isaiah 26:3-4, "Perfect Peace" collection. As I have mentioned in the other books, it started from how I drew near to the LORD in my workplace by keeping my mind on Him. Hallelujah!

I related numbers, you see throughout the day, everywhere, on almost everything on the LORD, His word, biblical events and facts. It's our desire for you to discover the power and presence of the Holy Spirit by relating a variety of things to the #11.

> **Remember**, the LORD Jesus <u>PROMISED us tribulation</u> while we were in this world.
> ***These things, I have spoken unto you,
> that in me ye might have peace.
> In the world ye shall have tribulation:
> But be of good cheer; I have
> overcome the world.***
> John 16:33 KJV

However, we have been <u>PROMISED His peace</u> while we endure these short trials, tribulations,

troubles, and tests. Perfect Peace is given only to those whose mind and heart recline upon the LORD. God's peace is increased in us according to the knowledge of His Holy Word.
Grace and peace be multiplied unto you through the knowledge of God, and of Jesus our LORD.
2 Peter 1:2 KJV

It's our hope that the #11 will forever means something unique, biblical and bring an unspeakable joy to your heart, when you see it, this day forward. Be Bless!

THANKS

I would like to say, as a disciple of the LORD Jesus Christ, we can rest assure that when we are seeking His plan and purpose for our lives, we will be successful because true success lies in doing His will; not in fame and fortune.

Remember, we may not know until we get to heaven just how much a book you suggested reading at the right moment have encourage a person to keep on going when a few minutes before they were tempted to give up on life, and maybe their walk with the LORD.

Thanks for Your Support . . .

ACKNOWLEDGEMENT

I would like to express my gratitude to **ALL** of God's people for making this possible. Remember . . . "God' gifts are still in YOU!"

For the gifts and calling of God
are without repentance.
Romans 11:29 KJV

For God's gifts and his call can
never be withdrawn.
Romans 11:29 NLT

Answer to a Question: *Explain Romans 11:29*

The Lord calls and gives every individual gift(s) to accomplish that call. Regardless of what that individual does, God doesn't withdraw His gifts and callings. When you live in sin you can't feel, see, hear, understand, or use the supernatural gifts of God flowing in your calling. You don't even have faith in your gifts. People who are living sinful lives are going to have their faith made shipwreck through their conscience, 1 Timothy 1:19.

**Cling to your faith in Christ, and
keep your conscience clear.
For some people have deliberately
violated their consciences;
as a result, their faith has been shipwrecked.**
1 Timothy 1:19 NLT

They lose effectiveness. However, the gifts and callings of God are still there and they will function because anything you have ever received from God is still there, it just needs to be activated by faith.

I hope and pray this helped you, along with others.
Dr. Vanessa

INTRODUCTION

For Those Who Want to be
Kept in "Perfect Peace"

This book was prepared and written to open your mind to a "Perfect Peace" that comes only from God. I'm striving to elevate you into a "Unique and Profound" awareness of God's presence around you at all time by using the #11.

According to some people, it is difficult to keep your mind on the LORD. While most Christians will agree that if you keep your mind stayed on the LORD, He will keep you in "Perfect Peace." You can experience His presence and peace throughout your day and every day.

This concept of this book was placed in my spirit by our Father, which art in heaven, to help me when He allowed Satan to test me at my workplace until he finished molding me.

Throughout these pages, I will be focussing on biblical events, and facts surrounding the #11. However, I am sure much more can be said on this, so these examples serve merely as an introduction and are not exhaustive by any means.

In the other books to follow, I will concentrate on another number, or set of numbers, or a passage of scripture. Be enlightened and enjoy the peace it will bring in Jesus' Name. Amen.

DEDICATION

I would like to dedicate this book to Missionary Donella Pierce Chambers' prayer line that helps me more than she will ever know.

CHAPTER 1

The #11

The #11 is associated with things that have the absence of organization, incompleteness and judgment. The word "eleven" is derived from the Old English word "endleofan," which means "one left," as in one left over ten. It is one beyond ten "the perfect number" which signifies completion and perfection of God's divine order and short of twelve, "the kingdom number" representing completeness in an organizational setting.

The #11 is used 24 times in the Bible, and the designation 11th is used 19 times in scripture. The first judgement executed upon mankind after the fall of man, resulted from Cain killing his brother Abel was executed in Genesis chapter four, verse eleven.

And now art thou cursed from the earth, which hath opened her mouth to receive thy brother's blood from thy hand;
Genesis 4:11 KJV

The second judgment was the flood of Noah's day. This judgement was executed in Genesis chapter seven, verse eleven.

**In the six hundredth year of Noah's life,
in the second month, the
seventeenth day of the month,
the same day were all the foundation
of the great deep broken up,
and the windows of heaven were opened.**
Genesis 7:11 KJV

Only two kings, reigned "eleven" years over Judah, and they both brought terrible judgment upon Judah. Jehoiakim reigned eleven years before Nebuchadnezzar's army carried Jerusalem into captivity, 2 Chronicles 36:5-9. In the eleventh year of Zedekiah, the last king of Judah, God executed His final judgment against Judah. Around 588 BC, Jerusalem was captured by Nebuchadnezzar, the temple burnt, the remaining Jews taken to Babylon, King Zedekiah blinded and taken into exile, and Judah reduced to a region control by the Roman Empire, 2 King 25:2.

At 9:03 pm, Central Time, February 8, 2014, feel the unction of the Holy Spirit say "Explain." Let me think? The first three kings of Israel were Saul, David and Solomon. After Solomon's death, the ten northern tribes revolted against his son Rehoboam. Israel divided into two sections/kingdoms named "Israel" and "Judah." Israel was in the north which consisted of ten of the twelve tribes, and Judah was in the south which consisted of two tribes. They had two different kings that ruled over them. The Israelites formed their capital in the city of Samaria, and the Judeans kept their capital in Jerusalem. Israel had 19 kings, and one was a queen to rule over them, and Judah had 20 kings to rule over them. These kingdoms remained separate for over 200 years. Around 722 BC, the Assyrians conquered Israel and forced the ten tribes to scatter throughout their empire. This is where the phrase "the ten lost tribes of Israel" come from. When Babylonians later conquered Judah around 586 BC, they also relocate the people but to a single location.

The number eleven also represent disorder and incompleteness. The judgement at Calvary was executed on the Lord Jesus Christ while there were "eleven" apostles. After Judas Iscariot had betrayed Jesus, he committed suicide leaving eleven disciples, Matthew 27:5. The disciples decided to replace Judas, even though, Jesus had been crucified. Judas was replaced by Matthias bringing the total back to twelve which is a "Kingdom Number" and it represents order and completeness compared to #11 which represents disorder and incompleteness.

MAY I ASK JUST ONE QUESTION? What book in the series speaks on the "Kingdom Number?" ANSWer iN back oF booK.

The journey of the Israelites through the wilderness from Horeb to Kadesh Barnea should have taken only eleven days, Deuteronomy 1:2. It turned into a 40-year journey because of the disorder, disorganization, and lack of faith.

According to Genesis 32, Jacob took his two wives, two maid-servants, and his eleven sons when they headed back home to confront his estranged brother Esau. At that particular time, Jacob had only eleven sons because Benjamin had not been born. Benjamin's birth brought the total of Jacob's son to twelve, the Kingdom number.

Joseph, Jacob eleventh son was sold into slavery, and Jacob thought Joseph was dead. This took the total back to eleven sons, during that period, much confusion characterized Jacob's household.

Joseph spent eleven years in Potiphar's household where disorder was caused by Potiphar's wife, and resulted in Joseph going to prison.

Other information concerning the #11 in regards to the Bible:

The Dukes of Edom were eleven in number, and these are the names of the Chief ("Dukes" in the KVJ Bible) of Esau, according to their families, after their places, by their names, Genesis 36:40-43.

1. Duke Timnah

2. Duke Alvah

3. Duke Jetheth

4. Duke Aholibamah

5. Duke Elah

6. Duke Pinon

7. Duke Kenaz

8. Duke Teman

9. Duke Mibzar

10. Duke Magdiel

11. Duke Iram

These are the names of the leaders of the clans of Edom. They all descended from Esau, the ancestor of the Edomites.

The eleven men of great authority were offended, when they were told the truth by one of God's servants are:

1. Pharaoh, Exodus 10:28

2. Balak, Numbers 24:10

3. Jeroboam, 1 Kings 13:4

4. Ahab, 1 Kings 22:27

5. Naaman, 2 Kings 5:12

6. Asa, 2 Chronicles 16:10

7. Joash, 2 Chronicles 24:21

8. Uzziah, 2 Chronicles 26:19

9. Jehoiakim, Jeremiah 26:21

10. Zedekiah, Jeremiah 32:3

11. Herod, Matthew 14:3

David had "eleven" Gadites that were brave and experience warriors from the tribe of Gad. They were experts with shields and spears. They were as fierce as lions, and swift as a deer on the mountains, 1 Chronicles 12:8-15.

1. Ezer the first was their leader

2. Obadiah the second

3. Eliab the third

4. Mishmannah the fourth

5. Jeremiah the fifth

6. Attai the sixth

7. Eliel the seventh

8. Johanan the eighth

9. Elzabad the ninth

10. Jeremiah the tenth

11. Machbanai the eleventh

The biblical Joseph was the 11th son of Jacob. He had eleven brothers. Let's name them:

1. Reuben

2. Simeon

3. L __ __ __

4. J __ __ __ h

5. Dan

6. Naphtali

7. G __ __

8. Asher

9. Issachar

10. Ze __ulu __

11. Benjamin, and there was a sister, Dinah

Need a little help? Look in the back of the book

Joseph dreamt the sun, the moon and 11 stars were bowing down to him, Genesis 37:9.

Joseph was 17 years old when he was sold into slavery, Genesis 32:7. He was 30 years old when Potiphar promoted him, Genesis 41:46; and spent two years in prison, Genesis 41:1. Joseph had been in Potiphar's house for 11 years before going to prison.

The Gospel of John records eleven unique promises.

1. A person can receive everlasting life by believing in the Son of God, John 3:16.

2. A person can have eternal life by eating, spiritually, Jesus' body, John 6:54.

3. By following Jesus you will not walk in darkness, John 8:12.

4. Those who continue in Jesus' word will be set free, John 8:31-32.

5. A person will truly be free if made so by Jesus, John 8:36.

6. God the Father will honor those who serve Christ, John 12:26.

7. Those who believe in Jesus will do greater deeds than he did, John 14:12.

8. Those who obey Christ's commands will receive the Holy Spirit, John 14:15 -16.

9. Those who keep Jesus' commands will be loved by both him and God the Father, John 14:21.

10. Those who abide in Jesus will be fruitful, John 15:5.

11. A person can be Christ's friend if they obey him, John 15:14.

Eleven different types of spices were used to make up the Ketoret. Ketoret is a Hebrew word which means "incense" in English. Ketoret is a substance which is associated with joy, prayer, and protection.

1. *Balsam

2. *Onycha

3. *Galbanum

4. *Frankincense

5. Myrrh

6. Cassia

7. Spikenard

8. Saffron

9. Costus

10. Aromatic Bark

11. Cinnamon

Note: The book of Exodus lists four components of the incense displayed by an *, but the Talmud lists seven additional components from the oral Torah.

The remaining apostles of Jesus were sometimes described as "the Eleven" even after Matthias was added to bring the total back to twelve, Acts 2:14.

The following phrases referring to our Saviour contain 11 letters:

1. God in Heaven

2. Our Redeemer

3. Jesus Christ

4. Saviour Jesus

5. Jesus is Lord

6. God Almighty

7. King of Kings

8. Lord of Lords

9. The Almighty

10. Bread of Life

11. Living Water

The #11 in regards to the world:

The 11th President of the United States is James Polk who served the country from 1845-1849. Polk was on the 11 cent stamp issued on September 8, 1938 in the Presidential Series.

World War I ended at the 11th hour of the 11th day of the 11th month.

Eleven is the numbers of guns in a gun salute to US Army, Air Force and Marine Corps Brigadier Generals, and to Navy and Coast Guard Rear Admirals Lower Half.

November 11 is Veterans Day in the United States, honoring military veterans.

South Africa has eleven official languages; Afrikaans, English, Ndebele, North Sotho, Swazi, Tsonga, Tswana, Venda, Xhosa, and Zulu.

The stylized Maple Leaf on the Canada flag has 11 points.

The first plane to hit the World Trade Center, North Tower on September 11, 2001 was American Airlines Flight 11. It had 92 on board and 11 were crew members. New York State is the 11th state of the US Constitution.

Apollo 11 was the first manned spacecraft to land on the moon. It was launched on July16, 1969 and the lunar landing was July 21, 1969. The difference between the lunar year and the solar year is exactly eleven days.

The record number of Oscar awards for any one movie is 11. This was achieved by both Titanic (1997) and Ben-Hur (1959), The Lord of the Rings: The Return of the King (2003).

American football team, a cricket team, a field hockey team, and most soccer teams are played with11 players on the field.

CHAPTER 2

The Dukes
of Edom

The words "Dukes of Edom" appear in the King James Bible four times. It first appears in the King James Bible as a name given by God to Esau's descendants, Genesis 32. The word "Duke" comes from the Latin word "dux" which means "a leader" and in Arabic it means "a sheik." This word is used in the Bible to denote the chief of the tribe. The name Edom means "red."

According to the Bible, Isaac and Rebekah had twin sons. Their names were Esau and Jacob. Esau was the first-born. He loved the outdoors and was a great hunter. Jacob was a plain person who dwelled in the tents.

Their mother Rebekah's favourite son was Jacob because he was a home-loving son while Isaac loved Esau. Esau was more like his father. He loved the outdoors, enjoyed hunting, and likes to eat of the venison he had killed.

One day, when Jacob was fixing some lentil soup, his brother Esau came in from the field tired and hunger. He asked his brother, Jacob for some soup because he was hunger. Jacob did not feed him at once but said, "Sell me first your birth-right, so that I may be like the elder son." Jacob won't give Esau any food until he agreed and sold his birth-right, then Jacob gave Esau bread and soup to eat.

When Isaac their father grew old, he was nearly blind. Soon after, he called his beloved Esau one day and said, "Take your bow and arrows, go out in the woods, and hunt some venison. Then roast it as I like it and bring it to me, so that I may eat and bless you before I die.

Rebekah heard Isaac talking with Esau. She wanted her husband last blessing to be for Jacob, who was her favourite. As soon as Esau left, she sent Jacob to bring her two kids from the flocks, and she prepared the savoury meat, roasted as Isaac loved it, and had Jacob bring it to him.

When Jacob brought the food to his father's bedside, he said, "I am Esau, your first-born son. I have done as you said. Sit up and eat, and then bless me." Isaac, thinking he recognized the voice as Jacob's, asked, "How did you find it so quickly?" And Jacob answered, "Because the Lord brought it to me."

Isaac, still doubting, said, "Come near that I may feel you and know whether or not you are really Esau." Rebekah had clothed Jacob in Esau's clothes, and she covered his smooth hands, wrists and arms with the skins of the lambs, so that they would feel very hairy like Esau. Isaac felt his hands, since he couldn't see, and said, "The voice sound like the voice of Jacob, but the hands feel like the hands of Esau."

Isaac eats the food and drinks the wine that Jacob gave him. Isaac then blessed Jacob with blessing that was meant for Esau.

**Therefore God give thee of the dew of heaven,
and the fatness of the earth, and
plenty of corn and wine:
Let people serve thee, and
nations bow down to thee:
be lord over thy brethren, and let thy
mother's sons bow down to thee:
cursed be everyone that curseth thee,
and blessed be he that blesseth thee."**
Genesis 27:28-29 KJV

Shortly after Jacob left his father, Esau returned from hunting and was ready to receive the blessing from his father. He finds out that Jacob had deceived their father and received his blessing. He vowed to kill Jacob as soon as Isaac died. Rebekah, their mother overheard this and order Jacob to travel to her brother Laban's house in Haran, until Esau's anger subsided.

Soon after, Esau married unbelieving Canaanite women. Their names were Adah, Oholibamah, and Bashemath, according to Genesis 36. His brother Jacob marries, their mother's brother daughters named Leah and Rachel.

What is Jacob's mother brother name?
. . . answer in the back of book

As I previously mentioned, "The Dukes of Edom" were eleven in number. They were loosely related to

Israel with different rules, order and government. A bitter hatred existed between them and Israel.

These were the name of the chief ("Dukes" in the KJV Bible) of Esau, according to their families and their places, by their names:

1. Chief Timnah,

2. Chief Alvah,

3. Chief Jetheth,

4. Chief Aholibamah,

5. Chief Elah,

6. Chief Pinon,

7. Chief Kenaz,

8. Chief Teman,

9. Chief Mibzar,

10. Chief Magdiel,

11. Chief Iram.

These were the chiefs of Edom, according to their dwelling places in the land of their possession. Esau was the father of the Edomities.

CHAPTER 3

Apple

What word is mentioned only 11 times in the King James Bible? It begins with an "A" and society says "it keeps the doctors away." It is believed to protect your immune system with Vitamin C, prevent heart disease with flavonoid, prevents various cancers, reduces bad cholesterol, protect your brain, prevent tooth decay and create healthier lungs. It's an "apple," and to my surprise it is not mentioned in the book of Genesis. So what fruit did Eve and Adam eat? . . . . . *smile*

And when the woman (Eve) saw that the tree was good for food, and that it was pleasant to the eyes, and a tree to be desired to make one wise, she took of the fruit thereof, and did eat, and gave also unto her husband (Adam) with her; and he did eat. Genesis 3:6 KJV

The word "apple" is mentioned mostly in the books of poetry which are Psalms, Proverbs, and Songs of Solomon. Apple is mentioned first in one of the five books of the law, Deuteronomy. The other books of the law are Genesis, Exodus, Leviticus, and Numbers.

He found him in a desert land,
and in the waste howling wilderness;
he led him about, he instructed him,
he kept him as the apple of his eye.
Deuteronomy 32:10 KJV

Next the word "apple" is mentioned in Psalm 17 which is a prayer by King David concerning protection against oppressors.

Keep me as the apple of the eye,
hide me under the shadow of thy wings.
Psalm 17:8 KJV

The word "apple" is recorded twice in the book of Proverbs, chapters 7 and 25. The Book of Proverbs provides remarkable wisdom on how to live a happy, joyful, successful, and peaceful life. Most of the writing of Proverbs has been credited to Solomon, the son of King David, the king of Israel.

Keep my commandments, and live;
and my law as the apple of thine eye.
Proverbs 7:2 KJV
A word fitly spoken is like apples
of gold in pictures of silver.
Proverbs 25:11 KJV

The word "apple" is mentioned four times in the book of Song of Solomon. The book of Song of Solomon consists of eight chapters concerning love.

As the apple tree among the trees of the wood,
so is my beloved among the sons.

**I sat down under his shadow with great delight,
and his fruit was sweet to my taste.**
Song of Solomon 2:3 KJV

**Stay me with flagon, comfort me with
apples: for I am sick of love.**
Song of Solomon 2:5 KJV

**I said, I will go up to the palm tree,
I will take hold of the boughs thereof:
now also thy breasts shall be
as clusters of the vine,
and the smell of thy nose like apples;**
Song of Solomon 7:8 KJV

**Who is this that cometh up from the
wilderness, leaning upon her beloved? I
raised thee up under the apple tree: there
thy mother brought thee forth: there she
brought thee forth that bare thee.**
Song of Solomon 8:5 KJV

Apple is then mentioned once in the selection of
books by the Major Prophets which are Isaiah,
Jeremiah, Lamentation, Ezekiel and Daniel.

**Their heart cried unto the LORD,
O wall of the daughter of Zion, let tears run
down like a river day and night: give thyself
no rest; let not the apple of thine eye cease.**
Lamentations 2:18 KJV

The last two times "apple" is mentioned is in the Minor Prophets' books.

**The vine is dried up, and the
fig tree languisheth;
the pomegranate tree, the palm
tree also, and the apple tree,
even all the trees of the field, are withered:
because joy is withered away
from the sons of men.**
Joel 1:12 KJV

**For thus saith the LORD of hosts;
After the glory hath he sent me unto
the nations which spoiled you:
for he that toucheth you toucheth
the apple of his eye.**
Zechariah 2:8 KJV

I wonder, can you name the other 10 Minor Prophets' books. Let's try:

1. Hosea

2. Joel

3. _____

4. _____

5. _____

6. Micah

7. _____

8. _____

9. Zephaniah

10. _____

11. Zechariah

12. _____

~ Need a little help, look in the back of the book ~

Note: The word "apple" is not mentioned in the New Testament.

CHAPTER 4

The Eleventh Hour

The expression "The Eleventh Hour" is the title of films, books and television episodes. It's the title of over 7 songs written from 1983 to 2011. There is also a haunted house attraction, a newspaper, and a video game named "The Eleventh Hour."

The Eleventh Hour refers to a point in time which is nearly too late. Other popular phrases that are associated with "The Eleventh Hour" are as follow:

1. The last moments just before a deadline

2. The last minute possible to render a decision

3. Just under the wire

4. Without a moment to spare

5. At the latest time possible

6. Running out of time

7. Procrastination

Vanessa Rayner

The reference to "The Eleventh Hour" was used by the Babylonians with their sundial. A sundial was divided into twelve-hour periods from dawn to sundown, so the eleventh hour came just before sunset. In other words, if you did something at "The Eleventh Hour," it was just before you ran out of daylight.

The eleventh hour was the last hour of sunlight with the twelfth hour bringing darkness. The English translation of "the eleventh hour" is "at five o'clock in the afternoon," Matthew 20:6.

And about the eleventh hour he went out,
and found others standing idle,
and saith unto them,
Why stand ye here all the day idle?
Matthew 20:6 KJV

"At five o'clock that afternoon
he was in town again
and saw some more people standing around.
He asked them, 'Why haven't
you been working today?'
Matthew 20:6 NLT

In reality, this expression originated from the Bible. The expression "the eleventh hour" means at the latest time possible. You'll find this concept used in Matthew 20:1-16, in the parable of the vineyard workers.

In fact, the only time the phrase "the eleventh hour" is used in the Bible in is the Gospel book of Matthew; the first New Testament Book. The eleventh hour is used in a parable told by Jesus, where a man had hired laborers at nine o'clock in the morning, at noon, then three o'clock and later hired some at the eleventh hour.

Despite the protests of those who had worked all day, those who came at the eleventh hour received a penny, just as those who had worked since early in the morning. Even though, the eleventh-hour worker only worked for an hour, they were paid the same wage as those who had worked all day.

Biblical scholars have suggested that the "Vineyard Workers Parable" Jesus told means that even people who come to Christianity late in life will still earn the full benefits of the joys of eternal life.

The Vineyard Workers Parables, Matthew 20:1-16

The Kingdom of Heaven is like the landowner who went out early one morning to hire workers for his vineyard. He agreed to pay them a denarius and sent them out to work.

At nine o'clock in the morning (the third hour) he was passing through the marketplace and saw some people standing around doing nothing. So he hired them, telling them he would pay them whatever was right at the end of the day. So they went to work in the vineyard. At noon (the sixth hour) and again at three o'clock (the ninth hour) he did the same thing.

At five o'clock that afternoon (the eleventh hour) he was in town again and saw some more people standing around. He asked them, why haven't you been working today? They replied, because no one hired us. The landowners told them go, and joins the others in my vineyard.

That evening he told the foreman to call the workers in and pay them, beginning with the last workers first. When those hired at five o'clock (the eleventh hour) were paid, each received a full day's wage. When those hired first came to get their pay, they assumed they would receive more. But they, too, were paid a day's wage. When they received their pay, they protested to the owner, those people worked only one hour, and yet you've paid them just as much as you paid us who worked all day in the scorching heat.

He answered one of them, Friend, I haven't been unfair! Didn't you agree to work all day for the usual wage? Take your money and go. I wanted to pay this last worker the same as you. Is it against the law for me to do what I want with my money? Should you be jealous because I am kind to others?'

"So those who are last now will be first then, and those you are first will be last."

CHAPTER 5

Eleven Spices

The Incense Offering was a sweet smelling perfumed offering. It was burnt on and altar called the "Golden Altar of Incense" in the time of the Tabernacle and the First and Second Temple period. It was an important ceremony performed by the priests in the Temple of Jerusalem.

0512   8/19/14   (I had a burning desire to explain Tabernacle, First and Second Temple) The Tabernacle was a portable dwelling place for the" Divine Presence of God." It was built by the specifications God revealed to Moses at Mount Sinai. It was used during the time of the departure of the Jews from Egypt through the conquering of the land of Canaan. Solomon's Temple is known as the First Temple in ancient Jerusalem built around 960 BC. The Second Temple was an important Jewish Holy Temple, which stood on the Temple Mount in Jerusalem during the Second Temple period, between 516 BC and 70 AD. It replaced the First Temple which was destroyed in 586 BC, when the Jews of the Kingdom of Judah went into exile under the Babylonian Captivity.

Eleven different types of Holy Spices were used to make the Incense Offering, also known as "Ketoret."

Ketoret is the Hebrew word for the English word "Incense." The word "Ketoret" means bonding.

The Ketoret was offered up twice a day to symbolized Israel's desire to serve "The Lord God" in a pleasing way. A total of five pounds of ketoret was burnt daily, half in the morning and half in the afternoon service. This occurs seven days a week, every day of the year on the Golden Altar of Incense, which sat in front of the curtain that separated the Holy Place from the Holy of Holies. The Golden Altar of Incense was smaller than the Brazen Altar.

Question Readers: *What was burned on the Brazen Altar? Back of book . . .*

The Golden Altar of Incense was a square with each side measuring 1.5 feet and 3 feet high. It was made of acacia wood and overlaid with pure gold. Four horns protruded from the four corners of the altar. God commanded the priests to burn incense on the Golden Altar every morning and evening, the same time that the daily burnt offerings were made.

And Aaron shall burn thereon
sweet incense every morning:
when he dresseth the lamps, he
shall burn incense upon it.
And when Aaron lighteth the lamps at
even, he shall burn incense upon it,
a perpetual incense before the LORD
throughout your generations.
Exodus 30: 7-8 KJV

God commanded the Israelites not to use this incense for any other purpose, or they would be cut off from their people, Exodus 30:37-38.

**Never use this formula to make
this incense for yourselves.
It is reserved for the Lord, and
you must treat it as holy.
Anyone who makes incense
like this for personal use
will be cut off from the community.**
Exodus 30:37-38 NLT

The incense was a symbol of the prayers and intercession of the people going up to God as a sweet fragrance.

The book of Exodus lists four components of the incense. However, the Talmud, which is a collection of ancient Jewish writings, lists seven additional components. The four components listed from the book of Exodus are Stacte (Myrrh), Onycha, Galbanum and Frankincense.

**And the LORD said unto Moses,
Take unto thee sweet spices, stacte,
and onycha, and galbanum;
these sweet spices with pure frankincense:
of each shall there be a like weight.**
Exodus 30:34 KJV

The eleven components of Ketoret are listed below with a brief description:

1. Balsam, the oil from the fruits is believed to have healing properties. The tree normally grows in the desert about 10 feet tall, bearing clusters of greenish flowers.

2. Cassia is the inner scented bark of an evergreen Asian tree that smells similar to cinnamon.

3. Cinnamon is a spice obtained from the inner bark of several trees from the genus Cinnamomum.

4. Cinnamon Bark comes from the tree thick gray bark.

5. Costus plant has large fleshly looking leaves and grows very quickly. The flowers are orange in color and the leaves are dark green and light purple. They are consumed by drying and grinding into powder.

6. Frankincense is tapped from the trees by stripping the bark, and allowing the resin to ooze out and harden.

7. Galbanum is an aromatic gum resin that comes from umbelliferous Persian plant species. They grow plentifully on the slopes of the mountain ranges of northern Iran.

8. Myrrh resin is a natural gum which comes from a number of small, thorny tree species of the

genus Commiphora. It has been used throughout history as a perfume, incense, oil and medicine.

9. Onycha (Clove), the onycha of antiquity actually cannot be determined with certainty. Some writers believe that onycha was the fingernail-like closing flap of certain sea snails.

10. Saffron is a spice derived from the flower of Crocus Sativus. It bears up to four flowers, each with three vivid crimson stigmas, which are the distal end of a carpel.

11. Spikenard is a historic class of an aromatic amber-colored essential oil derived from flowering plants. The oil has since ancient times been used as a perfume, as a medicine and in religious contexts.

CHAPTER 6

Eleven Letters

These well-known words come from the Bible, "God in Heaven," "Our Redeemer," "Jesus Christ," "Savior Jesus," "Jesus is Lord," "God Almighty," 'King of Kings," "Lord of Lords," "The Almighty," "Bread of Life," and "Living Water." They are viewed as titles of Jesus, our statement of faith, and phrases we say when we are praying to our Lord and Savior Jesus Christ. They are powerful, but also unique to me because they contain 11 letters.

1) God in Heaven:

The phrase "God in Heaven" is mentioned five times in the Bible, four times in the Old Testament, and once in the New Testament.

**Know therefore this day, and
consider it in thine heart,
that the Lord he is God in heaven above,
and upon the earth beneath: there is none else.**
Deuteronomy 4:39 KJV

**For in the resurrection they neither marry,
nor are given in marriage,
but are as the angels of God in heaven.**
Matthew 22:30 KJV

2) Our Redeemer:

Jesus is "our redeemer." He paid the price as our redeemer with His own blood. Jesus chose to die that we might live. The words "our redeemer" is only recorded twice and it's in the Old Testament book of Isaiah.

As for our redeemer, the Lord of hosts
is his name, the Holy One of Israel.
Isaiah 47:4 KJV

Doubtless thou art our father,
though Abraham be ignorant of us,
and Israel acknowledge us not:
thou, O Lord, art our father, our redeemer;
they name is from everlasting.
Isaiah 63:16 KJV

3) Jesus Christ:

The name Jesus is derived from the Hebrew - Aramaic word "Yeshua" meaning "Yahweh" the Lord is salvation. The name "Christ" is actually a title for Jesus. It comes from the Greek word "Christos" meaning "the Anointed One," or "Messiah" in Hebrew. The book of Matthew is the first place that we find the name "Jesus Christ" giving in the generation of our Savior, Jesus Christ.

The book of the generation of Jesus Christ,
the son of David, the son of Abraham.
Matthew 1:1 KJV

4) Saviour Jesus:

It's mentioned only in the New Testament seven times, starting with the book of Acts. Saviour Jesus can also be found in 2 Timothy 1, Titus 2, 2 Peter 2, 2 Peter 3, and twice in 2 Peter 1.

> **Of this man's seed hath God**
> **according to his promise**
> **raised unto Israel a Saviour, Jesus:**
> Acts 13:23 KJV

5) Jesus is Lord:

It means that He is the Supreme Ruler over all. The statement "Jesus is Lord" serves as a statement of faith for the majority of Christians who regard Jesus as both man and God. "Jesus is Lord" is only written twice in the NIV and NLT Bible. The King James Bible has "Lord Jesus."

> **If you openly declare that Jesus is Lord**
> **and believe in your heart that God**
> **raised him from the dead,**
> **you will be saved.**
> Romans 10:9 NLT

6) God Almighty:

The title "God Almighty" is written as "El Shaddai" in Hebrew. It means "God, the All-Powerful One." It's mentioned eleven times in the Bible, first in the book of Genesis in chapters 28, 35 43 and 48. It mentioned in Exodus 6, and the book of Revelation, six times.

**And God Almighty bless thee,
and make thee fruitful, and multiply thee,
that thou mayest be a multitude of people;**
Genesis 28:3 KJV

**And I saw no temple therein:
for the Lord God Almighty and the
Lamb are the temple of it.**
Revelation 21:22 KJV

However, the phrase "Almighty God" is only recorded three times in the Bible, Genesis 17, Ezekiel 10 and Revelation 19.

7) King of Kings:

The phrase "king of kings" is used six times in the Bible. Once, the phrase applied to God the Father, 1 Timothy 6:15, and twice to the Lord Jesus in Revelation 17:14 and Revelation 19:16. The other three times are in Ezra 7:12, Ezekiel 26:7, and Daniel 2:37, and refers to kings who expressed their absolute sovereignty over their respective countries.

8) Lord of lords:

The phrase "Lord of lords" is used five times in scripture, only referring to God. It's recorded in Deuteronomy 10:17, Psalm 136:3, 1 Timothy 6:15, Revelation 17:14, and Revelation 19:16.

9) The Almighty:

The title "the Almighty" appears forty-four times in the Bible, thirty-one times in the book of Job, and only once in the New Testament.

I am Alpha and Omega,
the beginning and the ending, said the Lord,
which is, and which was, and which
is to come, the Almighty.
Revelation 1:8 KJV

10) Bread of Life:

The phrase "bread of life" appears only twice in the Bible, and only in the Gospel of John in the sixth chapter. It is one of the seven "I Am" statements of Jesus.

And Jesus said unto them, I
am the bread of life:
He that cometh to me shall never hunger;
And he that believeth on me shall never thirst.
John 6:35 KJV

I am that bread of life.
John 6:38 KJV

Note: The seven *"I Am"* statements of Jesus from the Gospel of John:

I.   The Bread of Life

Jesus declared, "I am the bread of life. He who comes to me will never go hungry, and he who believes in me will never be thirsty." **John 6:35**

II. The Light of the World

Jesus spoke again to the people, he said, "I am the light of the world. Whoever follows me will never walk in darkness, but will have the light of the life." **John 8:12**

III. The Gate

I am the gate; whoever enters through me will be saved. He will come in and go out, and find pasture. **John 10:9**

IV. The Good Shepherd

"I am the good shepherd. The good shepherd lays down his life for the sheep." **John 10:11**

V. The Resurrection and the Life

Jesus said to her, "I am the resurrection and the life. He who believes in me will live, even though he dies; and whoever lives and believes in me will never die." **John 11:25-26**

VI. The Way, the Truth, and the Life

Jesus answered, "I am the way and the truth and the life. No one comes to the Father except through me." **John 14:6**

VII. The Vine

"I am the vine; you are the branches. If a man remains in me and I in him, he will bear much fruit; apart from me you can do nothing." **John 15:5**

11) Living Water:

The words "living water" is only in the book of John. It's written twice in John 4, and once in John 7. Jesus is the water that brings life to the soul. Just as the physical body needs water to live, so does man spirit. Jesus is the water needed by the spiritual part of man, and without it the soul will eventually die.

**HE that believeth on me,
as the scripture hath said,
out of his belly shall flow rivers of living water.**
John 7:38 KJV

AUTHOR'S CLOSING REMARKS

Even though, the #11 is described as a number that is associated with disorder, incompleteness and judgment; I still discovered wonderful things associated with it also. What you think? *Smile . . .*

> *He who kneels before God can stand*
> *before anyone, and against anything.*
> *May the "LORD of Peace," be*
> *with you and your family.*

Dr. Vanessa

REFERENCES

Chapter 1

1. The Meaning of the Numbers in the Bible: http://biblestudy.org/bibleref/meaning-of-numbers-in-the-bible

2. Bible Genealogy: http://complete-bible-genealogy.com/judah_israel_kings.html

Chapter 2

1. Holy Bible Dictionary: http://www.bible-dictionary.org/Duke

Chapter 3

1. 9 Reasons Why an Apple a Day Really Keeps the Doctor Away

   http://www.succeedwiththis.com/9-reasons-why-an-apple-a-day-really-keeps-the-doctor-away

Chapter 4

1. The Eleventh Hour: http://en.wikipedia.org/wiki/The Eleventh Hour

Chapter 5

1. Incense Offering: http://en.wikipedia.org/wiki/ Incense_offering

2. The Golden Altar of Incense: http:// the-tabernacle-place.com/articles/what is the tabernacle altar of incense

Chapter 6

1. Jesus Christ – Lord and Savior of the World: http:// christianity.about.com/od/newstestamentpeople/p/ jesuschrist.htm

ANSWERS:

Chapter 1
<u>Joseph's eleven brothers:</u>

1. Reuben

2. Simeon

3. Levi

4. Judah

5. Dan

6. Naphtali

7. Gad

8. Asher

9. Issachar

10. Zebulun

11. Benjamin, and there was a sister, Dinah

The 4th book:

Isaiah 26:3-4 "Perfect Peace IV" The Kingdom Number

Chapter 2
Laban

Chapter 3
1. Hosea

2. Joel

3. Amos

4. Obadiah

5. Jonah

6. Micah

7. Nahum

8. Habakkuk

9. Zephaniah

10. Haggai

11. Zechariah

12. Malachi

Chapter 5
The altar was the place for burning animal sacrifices.

OTHER BOOKS BY THE AUTHOR:

- From the Pew to the Pulpit published by iUniverse 08/29/07

- Isaiah 26:3-4 "Perfect Peace" published by AuthorHouse 09/07/10

- Isaiah 26:3-4 "Perfect Peace" The Last Single Digit published by AuthorHouse 02/10/2012

- Isaiah 26:3-4 "Perfect Peace III" Silver and Gold published by AuthorHouse 10/24/2012

- Isaiah 26:3-4 "Perfect Peace IV" The Kingdom Number published by AuthorHouse 04/10/2013

- Isaiah 26:3-4 "Perfect Peace V" 2541 published by AuthorHouse 09/06/2013

- Isaiah 26:3-4 "Perfect Peace VI" Zacchaeus published by AuthorHouse 02/25/2014